Dry Love

sobriety has taught me
there are a lot of good reasons
why i drank

poems by
CASH CARLOS

This book is dedicated to everyone who knows
the hell of addiction.

May you find your own way out of the darkness,
and live to tell the tale.

Cash Carlos

*I sat drinking liquor with fools,
when I should have been
having a cup of coffee with her.*

blackbird

my father drank and cheated
his entire life.
starting with my mother,
and continuing on with 2 more wives.
he never stopped cheating
until his death:
waitresses,
real estate agents,
video store clerks,
paralegals.
blondes,
brunettes,
redheads,
young,
and
old,
it didn't matter.
he drank, flirted,
and charmed his way
into their hearts,
but always found an excuse
to disappear into the horizon
like a blackbird at dusk,
until there was nothing left
but darkness and quiet.

As his son,
he left me no choice
but to get sober,
and stay faithful to one woman.

It was the only territory
left to explore.

some women

>Some women are like museums
>where you pay to enter
>and admire the frozen beauty on the walls,
>afraid to touch something by accident
>and ruin it
>with your dirty hands,
>but she was like an open field
>where you could fall in the tall grass
>and she would hold you
>exactly as you are.

princess

    She was a fussy fuck,
    full of spoiled perfections,
    a dirty princess untangling her hair
    by moonlight,
    and I thought I could spread her out
    on a peasant's blanket,
    feed her fruits,
    and cheap wine,
    and she'd be content
    with sweets, poetry, bone,
    and the promise of miracles by midnight,
    but she wouldn't be tamed by such mortal magic,
    and eventually grew tired
    of my pauper ways.

    She turned her body into a tattoo
    of a mermaid on my arm,
    and her soul into the crumbling salt
    at the top of my tequila glass.

a bed, a tv, and a bong

At first I thought
love could be as simple
as a bed,
a TV, and a bong,
and I delivered it all
to you with a smile
until the rent was due,
and you said
I was not a man.
You said I had let you down.
You said love
could not find a way
if I could not find the rent.

And so I learned
love is more than a bong hit
and big ideas:
it means getting up with the sun
to sell shoes to strangers,
just so you can afford to stay in one place;
it means reading the space
between words
and wishes.

it's knowing love won't last
without dedication,
resources,
and a much bigger plan.

ghosts

So many nights,
we'd be together
in the same room
doing different things,
like two ghosts
dissolving
into the wallpaper,
and coming out
only when
they were hungry.

vodka

She was a strawberry blonde alcoholic
with the best ass in blue jeans I'd ever seen.
She'd lived in Paris, and Rome,
and had a trust fund from her dead father,
a man she said she hardly knew.
She was like a bee dipped in wild honey;
she liked to make me jealous
by flirting with every man in the bar;
and it worked; "It's time to go home,"
I'd say, "I have got a stomach ache."
"I'm having fun," she'd say,
twisting her perfect ass into somebody's lap
and laughing, but I didn't find it funny.

Liquored up,
with cheap vodka in her veins,
her heart was an open wound,
and she would spill it everywhere,
but mostly on me.

And so to make a short story
even shorter,
let me just say we didn't last long
because a man needs
somebody who can stay in place longer than a dance,
somebody who doesn't have one eye on the door,
somebody who can slow down long enough to listen.

The only time i wrote her a poem,
she looked at it like she was looking at a ketchup label
or a laundry list; "Ah," she said, "that's sweet,"
as she twist toward the doorway
in a dress with no panties
looking for bigger fish to fry,
or some fresher metaphor
that still wouldn't work to describe her,
because she was more than strawberry blonde hair,
good looks and rhythm.

There was a fire in her heart,
and enough vodka
in her tank
it was only a matter of time
before it exploded.

And why not say it?

This is a time in my life
when I wouldn't have wanted it
any other way,
as I counted the minutes
on the clock
and waited for the fuse
to find its end.

cowboy boots

there was a moment
that summer,
when it was all going to hell;
we were at a gas station
outside of Portland, Oregon,
still not speaking to each other
and she was getting
into the car,
and her tan and dusty legs
sticking out of the car door
looked like the most
beautiful things
i'd ever seen,
but i could not tell her
because we'd been fighting
for so long over nothing,
and everything,
i had forgotten how to be
anything
but an asshole,
and so i write this poem,
now,
twenty years too late,
to say,
i have forgiven myself
for everything,
including this.

college dropout

i flunked math
and love,
and wandered
for years like a blind man
among the clouds and the vagrants,
searching for answers
to questions in my heart,
but my mistakes
stuck to me like tarred feathers,
and i felt like a ridiculous bird,
afraid to fly;
I knew
my wings were too heavy to take flight,
so I sang
loudly from my cage,
but never left the ground.

It took me a long time to learn
the sooner
you can forgive yourself,
the sooner you can say,
"fuck it, i did what i could do
with what i had,"
and that flying
is just another name
for getting your shit together
and moving on.

inspired

Once,
in the tornado of youth,
i wrote a girl a love poem
on the back of a sales receipt
that said, "She was a gypsy
with eyes that saw everywhere
and everything
and nowhere was home."
Years later she told me
she kept it to this day,
tacked to her wall
to remind her.
And when I asked her
of what, she said,
"There are only
a few people
in this world
who have eyes
to see all of you,
and you
were
always
one."

the professional loser

I saw my brother was suffering,
so I wrote him a poem,
explaining how his life was an illusion,
that working 24/7 to purchase products
that collected dust in his garage
was no way to reach Nirvana
in this lifetime or any other.
"You're right," he said, looking up at me
in wonder. "I have been
a slave in gold chains, suckling mindlessly
at the teat of empire, and I know not
what I do."

He quit his job the next day,
picked up painting, and met a woman
with a foreign accent
who taught him the pleasures of peaches,
and staying in bed on Sunday.
He downsized his car to a bicycle,
and got passed by fancy cars on the freeway,
all heading to the same hell he just escaped.

Feeling sorry for them,
he made a hundred copies of the poem
and put them in the breakroom by the coffee machine,
hoping to liberate his coworker's one soul at a time,
until there would be nobody left
to work the machines or punch in the clock,
but even in a perfect world,
he could still see
that one lonely bastard
who never got the deeper meaning,
standing in an empty boardroom,
scratching his diamond-studded balls,
and wondering where everybody went.

Is that you?

addictions

By 26, I was done drinking.
tired of waking up with a bottle in my hand,
tired of not being able to feel anything
but the ceaseless craving for more.
And so I turned to weed,
hoping it could save me from myself
like a dark green jesus with a gospel
of smoke and fire, but it no longer held
the same truth it did in my youth
when I could laugh at a lemon
and eat peanut butter forever;

The preacher inside my head
made me go crazy,
as I saw things that weren't there.
I heard voices singing opera in the rain,
and saw devils holding devil puppets above me.
I knew I couldn't run any longer
from my feelings, and
I would have to face the world
without a hammer or a crutch.

I remember I walked out of my door
on my first day truly sober.
It was snowing,
and i didn't know
if I was hot or cold
or if this was beauty or disaster,

but I knew I felt alive,
and open to the living sunlight,
with no place left to go but here.

existentialism for beginners

Here is the problem
with life always happening
in the moment:
when it's good, it's good,
but when it's bad,
it's worse than bad
because not only
do you have to deal
with whatever shit
you're dealing with at the time,
but then you've got to clean up
all the dirty chemicals
that flood a human brain
when they are down on their luck.
And this is when they will tell you
to breathe deeply, go jogging,
and eat right,
or these chemicals will color
everything you do,
past, future, and present,
the color of shit.

They warn that you will forget how it felt
when the sun shined,
the toilet worked,
and the good times
seemed like they would go on forever.

And so life turns us all
into joggers,
and plumbers,
and sailors who can weather
the shit storms,
riding the tide until morning
when the coast is clear
and the sun rises again
over the dark
and homely water.

the fisherman

My sister
is in a constant state of self-improvement,
with yoga, positivity, and prayer,
and last week at the art exhibit,
she said she didn't like the negative energy
of the paintings,
and that she preferred sunlight
and skiing,
and long walks along the sand.

I laughed,
because I understood
what she was saying,
and I knew I couldn't explain
to her
why I was so moved
by this dark painting
of a fisherman lost in the waves
or how I found
hope
in the sadness of the sea.

We both had the same alcoholic father,
who drank himself to death too soon,
and if he was the sailor in the storm,
I'd say she wanted to love him
by forgetting his suffering,
and I wanted to love him
by remembering.

lines for laura

    i had just turned 17,
    when me and this girl from English class
    drove to the top of the hill overlooking the city,
    and we drank tequila from paper cups,
    as the sun filled us up
    with what the tequila couldn't.

    i don't remember
    what i said to make her laugh,
    but i remember
    how i went from wanting to kiss her,
    to just wanting to remember this moment,
    as something beautiful and rare,
    so i watched the wind blow through her hair,
    and sunlight catch her smile,
    and i took a picture of her
    with my soul,
    and kept it with me,
    like all the best lines of poetry.

make it through

There's always somebody
going mad, dying too soon,
somebody lost,
somebody lonely,
somebody broken
like an antique jar collecting dust.
And everyone is just trying to make it through,
with pills and candy bars,
with whiskey bottles
and football.
Make it through with scrapbooks
and TV.
Make it through with country music,
porn, and dried flowers.
Make it through with poetry or cocaine
or new shoes from the mall.
Some put on boxing gloves,
and some collect butterflies,
or play video games
Some hold crucifixes like lucky dice.
Some make it through
with tattoos and greeting cards,
some chop onions, and others
believe in conspiracies about Elvis,
and JFK. Time passes,
and everyone wants to feel
like they're something special under the sun,

but sooner or later everybody feels
lost and lonely,
and looks for something
to love enough
to make it through.

procrastination

Our apartment was always
a wreck,
and we liked it that way.

it gave us a reason
to believe
getting our lives together
was only
a few dishes away.

karma sutra

All she wanted was to smoke and have sex,
which lasted for a while
because she had
the mind of an astronaut
and the body of a pearl diver,
but she wasn't interested
in my philosophical discussions,
which she called "mental golf,"
and I wasn't interested
in her scientific formulas
to explain the world in numbers,
but she was also well read
in the Tibetan art of pleasure,
and as voracious as a tiger in the wild,
so I had to ask myself: how many nights
will a man lie in bed in the sleepy buzz
of nothingness, lazily stroking
a perfect ass in the dark,
even if it belongs to a stranger?

The answer is many more
than you think,
but the exact number
is still God's private mystery.

good books

i go looking for books
like i'm looking for a fucking date.
i try not to judge them by their covers,
and first lines, but most of the time
i can tell by the first corny sentence
that the night will not go well between us;
other times I will read a paragraph or two,
before I realize I like their style,
but there wasn't enough substance
to meet again for coffee.

Only very rarely do I find a book
that is both funny and sad,
witty and profound,
yet humble, and real enough
for me to be willing to put in the time
to make it to the end,
amazed there could be
another person on earth,
who appreciates the same madness,
the same fleeting beauty,
the same triumphs and losses,
the same absurdity and despair as i do.
And even after it's done,
and i put the book on the shelf
beside the others,
i will continue to smile to myself
when i see it

Cash Carlos

like an ex lover you pass on the street
because you know something real passed between you,
and even if it didn't last forever,
you will always be grateful for it
because life is short,
and the number of shitty books out there
so very very long.

shakespeare and company

The most beautiful girl i knew in school
had her mother's mad green eyes,
eyes that spoke of broken promises
and dreams of a tomorrow that never comes.

She kissed me once at a party
when I wasn't expecting it,
and told me, "I can't love you forever,
only for a day."

I laughed, because she really spoke like that,
in poetry, and honestly believed that romance
would always overcome.

She wrote in a diary constantly
about all the places she would go,
like Bali, Toyko, and Paris
and I would just smile as she spoke,
because I admired her passion,
even if it was only a poet's dream.

I kept in touch with her over the years,
first when she was married and lived on a farm.
then when she was divorced with a child,
then doing porn to make a living,
then addicted to meth and losing her child
to the state before she met a man
with enough money to take her to Europe.

Cash Carlos

i don't know what happened to him
or her daughter, but the last time she wrote me
to say she now lives by herself in Paris,
where she's writing the story of her life.

The letter came with a photograph of her
standing in front of a famous old bookstore,
and she is smiling the way she used to smile,
when she told me she was going places
i wouldn't believe were true.

golden goose

What the fuck is wrong with me?
I complain for years about being broke,
downtrodden, and down on my luck,
then along comes this stunner
like a golden goose.
Born to a family of dentists and doctors,
she's got perfect teeth
and a private school education;
she looks likes the cover of a yoga magazine,
and talks like a literary journal.
She says she loves my sense of humor
and the way I write; she says
I make her feel "alive,"
and instead of taking the compliment
and running with it all the way to the bank
to live the happily ever after,
I hear myself saying, "Well, I guess
compared to all those well-bred dullards
you're used to,
I must be quite an amusement,
quite a thrill."

And so,
instead of being kind,
shutting my mouth,
and taking my ticket
to the promised land,

I questioned her motives,
and pushed her away.

I told her she wouldn't be happy
with a guy like me,
and just like a prophet
who can predict his own poverty,
and pain,
I was right.

for richer or for poorer

one month you're eating out,
and tipping extra to the table,
and the next day you can't pay the bills,
as the mind narrows like a stone
you want to throw at the universe
for being such a cheap bastard,
but the universe is too big to be insulted,
and laughs.

it knows there are men walking in space,
killers out on parole,
roses filled with agony,
and snow filled mountains
where nobody will tread,
and so your anger is reduced
to humility and shame,
as you know everything matters
as much as nothing,
and there are those in this world
who can hardly afford to breathe.

But I imagine even the poorest on this planet
must have faith in something,
a dog, a taco, a smile,
or else why keep on working.
fucking.
fighting, and sticking to a plan,
if you can't even afford
to cry.

Even when the day finally comes
when I can pay the heating bill again,
instead of being happy,
I'm slightly pissed at how little
it changes anything,
because I am still me,
for richer or for poorer,
and the best part of my day
was walking to the post-office
with nothing on my mind but sunlight.

the hole

We fucked for 40 days and 40 nights
and talked until the moon was full
and the liquor ran dry,
but it wasn't enough to fill the hole
that exists between two people
born on the opposite sides of the tracks,
mine with low rent and broken windows,
and hers with a golf course, gates,
and clubhouses as white as snow,
and when it ended,
it ended in fierce tears of rage,
and desperation,
not only for us,
but for an entire world
that is broken in two by the same tracks,
and searching for the same impossible love
that never seems to last longer
than that corny love song that played on the radio,
on the day you first met.

bones

Greasy fingers
and fried chicken,
she grabbed my cock
in the front seat of the car,
and said, "I want a bone,"
and I was in love
with this girl
and she was in love with me,
and our bellies were full,
and we were young,
and we pulled over
to the side of the road,
and had a quickie,
as the box of chicken
knocked over
spilling bones,
crispy legs,
and gravy,
and summer
was never as simple
or beautiful
again.

white ferrari

I'm part Latin, part Irish,
a dangerous mix of historically oppressed peoples
who have drank themselves to death
in the wake of failed revolutions;
My Irish mother still eats a thousand miles an hour,
afraid the food will run out forever,
and my Colombian father drank himself to death
 in the middle of the American Dream.
He lost his house by the lake,
and ended up with nothing
but a rope tied around his waist for a belt.

I've been driving shitty cars since I was 16,
telling myself on the daily, at least I have got a fucking car
because I know there are fields full of children
who will never know the joy
of blazing down the highway above 55 on a Sunday.

And even though I have a sunroof on my dented Subaru,
I don't open it. I am afraid it is too much luxury
for one man to take, and unfair to somebody else
who wasn't lucky enough to have been born
inside the Death Star that never sleeps.

My empire-guilt doesnt help anyone, including me,
and there are a million self-help gurus out there
telling me to open up my window and let in the breeze.

Then get a bigger car to show the world
how much of a badass you can be,
but I am afraid power and luxury
are just two more addictions
I will have to kick in order to stay sane.

So I keep my sunroof closed
sometimes to remind myself
I am just as happy with my window open,
and nobody can tell me otherwise.

But who am I talking to
when I saw a kid today who looked barely 16,
as he passed me in a white Ferrari
on the freeway.

His sunroof was open, and he was smiling,
eyes almost closed,
as if he were talking directly to God.

moby dick is dead

I wanted to be a novelist,
until I saw everybody on the bus
staring at their phones,
and realized nobody
wants to read a novel anymore,
not even me,
and I wanted to be a fucking novelist!

Because now, with 24/7 entertainment
streaming from the hinterland
in real time,
there are people jumping from bridges
for followers,
and people lighting themselves on fire
just to get the attention
their parents never gave,
just to escape the 9 to 5.

And now the world gets to watch
the whole madhouse
go up in flames
from the comfort of our own phones.

Meanwhile, the novelist
waits for somebody to open his book
and read, "It was the best of times, it was the worst of times,"
but the book stays on the shelf collecting dust,

and our brains explode in scattered particles
of self-help quotes, memes,
and DIY porno.

When entertainment is the purpose of life,
it is only a matter of time before the circus clowns
become suicidal,
so why bother reading
when everybody knows it is the best of times,
and the worst of times,
because they're living it.

edibles

Stoned as a rat bird,
I come down with conspiracy fever,
as I deciphered the lines
on a Coke can as the thinly veiled
all-seeing-Eye of the Illuminati,
that powerful, yet secretive group
rumored to run the world
through branding,
secret handshakes,
and cash,
but this was before the internet,
so nobody would believe me.

Not even my mother who hung up on me,
saying, "Get off the dope."

Not my father who said, "Son, ju
are talking crazy, and ju need to have a drink."

Not even the pizza guy who came to my house,
who just shook his head when I told him,
as if nothing were wrong,
as if the pizza slice
shining on the top of his car
in the shape of a pyramid
wasn't all part of the plan
to keep us shackled with bad ideas,
and always hungry for more.

bus station

She drank alone
in her room,
hoping somebody
would find her there,
and save her from herself,
but when she realized
nobody was coming,
and all the princes
were made of paper,
and all the horses
had been put to sleep,
she put down the bottle,
and started walking
toward the same dimly lit bus station
at the edge of town
where everybody's life begins.

*Sometimes you can look back on a relationship
and see the exact moment
when you agreed to take each other to brink of hell,
and still you wouldn't take it back
for the world,
because it taught you to respect the fire.*

top 40

This one liked sex and drugs
and top 40 music
that went boom, boom, boom,
and because her body
was like a theme park
where all the rides went upside down,
I tried to keep up with her,
but she just kept wanting more,
more lights, more music, more smoke,
more pills, more glitter, more applause,
and I began to feel ancient, worn out,
wondering where all this would lead,
but her body and the music kept me
from thinking about it too hard
with its boom, boom, boom,
so we stayed together
far longer that we would have
had she had been into classical music,
the kind that allows a man to reflect
on why he's still up at 6 am,
watching the sun rise over the city
like a broken chandelier.

bad news

There has always been bad news,
but never have we had access
to such up-to-date shit kicking misery
as we do now;
we've got real-time charts and graphs
showing us the global misery scale
and we read it
late into the night,
hoping we don't fall into the abyss;
we inhale stories of murder and madness
like electric cocaine.
we inject injustice
and lies into a blood until it boils,
our hearts sink,
and our bodies go limp.
we try to sleep
but we can't
because we know
we're just contributing more
to the rise in misery,
just by thinking about it,
and so it goes,
until eventually you learn
you can't give much of a fuck
about anything
but what is right in front of you,
and even that seems
more than enough
for any human to face.

tangerine

she's eating a tangerine,
as the sunlight runs through her hair,
and the birds shake on the roof,
and she doesn't know i notice her,
eating a tangerine,
peeling the skin,
and plucking each piece of fruit
with her fingers,
because sometimes i write poetry
in silence,
poetry just for me,
but this one
is for me, and you.

To remind us
there is magic in simple moments,
even on a rainy Tuesday
when the rent is due,
and we don't have it.

pink flamingos

A cheap hotel in Vegas
with neon pink flamingos,
and the air a hot, glittering dust,
I was trying to figure out
why I was alone again:
she was here a moment ago
laughing like the sun
and filling up the desert with her laughter,
her questions, her gentle touches,
and sweet songs,
and maybe it was something I said
or didn't say that sent her packing,
as if words were the only thing on earth
God created to keep love in one place,
while the rest of the world falls apart,
because I never cheated on her,
I never lied,
but still she was gone
like the Roman Empire,
like DB Cooper,
like Jesus
like Dinosaurs
like yesterday,
and I was still there,
studying my heart like a history book
full of unanswered questions,
trying to figure out
how to glue us back together
when all the best chapters
had now been torn in two,
and blew like tumbleweeds in the wind.

zen high

Whereas some mediate by closing their eyes,
and focusing on the breath and nothing else,
I meditate with my eyes open,
writing down the words as they come,
sometime vapid, sometimes fierce,
a cow ambling down a runway,
a pigeon exploding on the rocks.
And I do not know if I am ignorant or wise,
only that I am afraid of the peaceful
and vacant eyes
of those who meditate on blankets
and come back to report
they've seen the other world
and it is as calm and lovely
as a Holiday Inn California,
where old couples in golf shirts
make small talk about the weather,
because it is always nice
and sunny where they live,
yet somehow always the same.

I prefer to meditate on the free breakfast,
the coffee, and the waffle machine,
where all you have to do is pour in the batter
and wait for the miracles to happen.

humble pie

Once you've felt your heart
stabbed, and emptied
like a bag of sugar
on the ground.

Once you've wandered around like a blind man
walking into walls,
people,
and doors,
you know you can survive anything.

After that,
all your bad days are relative,
and even the slightest grain of sweet
will taste like an ice cream sundae.

poetry is for pussies

I haven't met a guy that reads poetry since college,
and then it was mostly Bukowski because he was drunk.
And i think it is because so many poets today
write about flowers and the moon,
men think it's just another man
trying to get a girl into the sack,
which it usually is,
and so women continue reading poetry
looking for love between the pages,
and making connections between words and feelings
while men forget how to speak from the heart,
and their words wither and die like old grapes.

And I think it may be too late to save us.
The TV has won. The beer has won.
The ball games have won.
The porno has won.

And I don't blame the men,
I blame the poets for abandoning them
like their fathers.
for writing poems to get published
and praised,
for writing to get accolades and applause
instead of just admitting
we've been utter fools most of our lives,
and are afraid to be alone.

We've left men to their vices
and death,
and they have forgotten
what it's like to hear themselves
in another man's voice
without feeling like a pussy.

Pussy is the word men use
to tear down other men,
straight or gay,
rich or poor,
high or sober,
anyone
who is still capable
of feeling,
as if feeling were a disease
caught only by women.

No wonder men don't read poetry.

No wonder they have to drink to feel.

No wonder they die broken by things
they can't explain.

a's are failures

My father drove drunk most of the time,
and we'd listen to Latin music,
him singing, and me not knowing
what to say.

Sometimes I pretended
to sing along with him in Spanish to show my love;
other times I just looked blankly out the window.

He loved me, but the horror of his childhood
left him broken and blind to me.
He saw only the parts of who I am that related to him,
and couldn't help telling me
the same terrible things his father told him.

Once, I brought straight A's home from school
to prove I could be smart like him, and he said,
"Son, you can bullshit jour teacher,
jourself and the entire juniverse, but ju cannot
bullshit me."

"But, Dad," I said, "I got straight A's."

My father took a drink of his scotch,
and said, "Son, A's are a failure."

It was in this moment
I realized there was nothing on earth
I could do to please my father,
and I was free from having to pretend
otherwise.

Now years later, after his death,
I am a sober father,
trying to give my son everything my father couldn't give me,
like time and attention,
and unconditional love.

When my son brings home good grades,
I congratulate him,
tell him to keep it up,
but another part of me can't help thinking that
there's some truth to what my father said,
and that just going by the rules
and being a workaholic is no way to go either,
so I tell my son to relax,
do his homework another day.

We skip school to go skateboard
in an abandoned parking lot
because I know these are the things
a son remembers more
than another day doing drills in school,
and time passes so quickly
between a father and a son,
you have to grab it when you can.

We listen to rap music all the way home,
and even though I can hardly understand a word,
I try to sing along anyway
because it makes me feel alive,
and like we're all in this together.

summer

The sun was falling, but it was still too hot to go outside.
It was summer in your apartment.
We had only been together a few weeks,
but i remember looking at you
and thinking you had everything
i could want in a woman,
brains, body, laughter, and style.

It was the way you carried yourself across the room,
the way you spoke of books, politicians,
and movies--that fleeting sunlight,
and you in it,
still stays with me like a dream.

It's been years now
since we've been together,
but i keep these memories of you
with me like an old mixtape
marked "US" in a magic marker,
and I play it whenever
I hear the earth is on fire,
because it reminds me of that summer,
and how lucky I am to still have you
walking with me through the flames.

curtains

    yesterday i caught a glimpse of the neighbor lady naked,
    because she left her curtain open
    directly in front of where I park,
    and though i happened to get glimpse of her tits,
    i was not aroused,
    and kind of saddened that I wasn't aroused.

    The next morning when i saw her
    getting into her car,
    i waved at her
    with a sad look
    as if to say,
    well, at least we tried.

l.a. woman

I sit writing this poem on a rainy day in Seattle,
and sometimes on days like this,
I wonder if I'd be doing the same thing in L.A.
where it is always sunny,
and there are girls in bikinis and movie stars
and lights that never dim.

The last time I was in L.A. I was only twenty two
and going out with a girl named Anne
who had just moved there from Seattle
to make it as an actress;
she was brunette, stylishly dressed,
from a wealthy family.

All her life she'd been taught to be bold,
confident and unafraid,
which is why I always wondered
what she saw in me,
other than a wit to match hers,
and a love of Spanish poetry.

I believed in her,
and thought she could make it
if anyone could, but I didn't
have the ambition
to be famous beyond my friends,
so I stayed in Seattle,
but still came down on weekends when I could.

Cash Carlos

She always loved to drink and party with me,
but at some point she developed a coke problem
and then the need to keep up her habit
by stripping at a club called Candy's Place.

All of this she told me on our last visit,
when my stomach dropped through the floor,
and it felt like she had died.

At the bus station,
she told me it was over, said I was too good
for her, and I laughed because I was the one
who talked her into her first line of coke,
and for a moment it felt as if we were in a movie,
and that all the tears smearing her face
with make-up weren't real,
and that somebody was going to say, "cut,"
and tell us we did a good job.

I wanted her to smile like she used to smile
when she still had daylight in her eyes,
but the night was coming too fast.

I boarded the bus,
hoping she'd come with me as the credits rolled,
but by the time I looked out the window,
she was already walking in the other direction,
and the only thing that followed me home
was the rain.

glazed donuts

my roommate is high as fuck,
his eyes like glazed donuts,
drool falling down the right corner of his mouth;
he thinks he is having a good time,
that this is really living,
but his pleasure centers are so stimulated,
he can't move,
and he reminds me of a sea urchin
in a tide pool.

later, he will begin to stir,
and motivate himself to put on a movie,
usually about drug lords or documentaries on food.
but, then he lights up again
to "enjoy it more."

Finally, he will fall asleep again
with the same look on his face
as he had when he was awake,
thinking, "This is the life."

road trip

    enlightenment playing golf on Sunday
    enlightenment taking acid in the desert
    enlightenment fucking in a closet
    enlightenment shadow boxing
    enlightenment reading literature
    enlightenment pissing on a dumpster
    enlightenment driving through the desert
    enlightenment watching TV
    enlightenment eating tacos
    and tasting the flavor
    of eternity
    in just one second.
    "THIS IS SOME GOOD SHIT,"
    you say, stuffing your face
    until the flavor fades
    in the sunlight,
    but you keep eating more,
    hoping to capture
    that original taste,
    but it never arrives,
    because you are no longer
    in the moment,
    and can only find the fat echo
    of what was once bliss.

    "You have to let it happen,"
    the gurus tell you,
    getting rich
    by saying the same thing
    you could have learned
    for the price of a taco.

billy

When you're younger,
you don't realize how most of the people
you're meeting are temporary,
passing through your life like ghosts;
like Billy the Native American drifter
who stayed with us for a while on Garden Street,
sustaining himself mostly on canned beans
from the food bank. He had black hair
and infections laughter that reminded me
of all of my crazy Colombian uncles.

Over black coffee,
he explained to me the difference
between heaven and hell
form his Native perspective;
"Hell," he said, "is like this can of beans,"
and he cracked a can on the counter
to show hard it was, and dead.

"Now," he said, "look at this cat,"
as he put his hand up to our cat's face.
"See how it moves, and reacts. it's alive,
and that is heaven."

I thought I understood
what he meant, but then
he started telling me how
he was being hunted by the CIA

for black ops done overseas,
and I didn't know if he was telling
the truth or not,
but a week later he disappeared
and I never saw him again.

Thinking back now,
I wonder if it really matters.
To be alive is to be alive,
and to be dead is to be dead,
and even if the CIA was
only in his own mind,
something was hunting him,
and he had to move like a cat
in order to stay alive,
because everything ends up
being a metaphor in the end.

Billy was a ghost
who stayed with us for a while,
then left,
only to return again
to haunt me
in the form of this poem
about heavenly cats
and the hell of canned beans.

ignorant art

Stone cold sober
I went looking for women
the way I did when I was drunk,
but it wasn't the same.
I couldn't convince myself
I wasn't bothered by things
that the booze would always forgive,
and so I remained single
and sober for a long time.

I have always had a thing for shitty art,
art scribbled by children
and madmen,
paint splattered across
the canvass with sincerity
and grit; and I hate the gimmick,
the pre-planned work of charlatans
who crave celebrity
and fame. And sometimes
it can be hard to tell the difference.

It is all in the gut,
I suppose,
so that is why I said no
to the beautiful girl I met at the gallery
who liked Rimbaud and foreign movies,
and long walks by the sea.

Everything looked good on paper,
but there was something
about her beautiful
and eager face,
and the perfection of her eyelashes
that told me she wouldn't forgive me for my messes,
and my love of fast food.

Sometimes I wanted Neruda and Yeats,
but most of the time I wanted tacos,
boxing, and to be left alone,
so it must be the the classical part of me
that still sings of her beauty,
even if I left her like a painting hanging on the wall
where I was sure somebody else
would buy it.

twenty one

She was reading a book of poetry.
she was dressed in black.
she was full of promise.
i was hungover,
smoking a cigarette
and trying to be poetic in real life.

I was lost.
I was confused.
I was trying to read
a book of philosophy,
hoping I could straighten out the world
with one good theory,
but the world
was already too far bent and broken
and my father was far too drunk
for me to fly in a straight line,
and so i looked at this girl
reading a book of poems
and I wondered
if she'd found the answer
in poems,
and if that is why
she looked so sultry
reading in the corner,
even though
she was dressed
in black.

Cash Carlos

I wanted to be a romantic back then,
but I knew she was only an image of hope,
and I was only a dreamer
looking for another drug
to wipe the darkness from my eyes,
and let me see color again.

the sadness of pancakes

i don't know why i fucked her,
this fully flavored blonde
I met at the movies.
I didn't know if it was loneliness,
alcohol or the way she could quote Marcuse,
but i knew it was anything but love,
and so when she came out of the bathroom,
still naked with tangled hair,
i didn't want to look at her.

She asked me if I wanted pancakes,
and for some reason,
this made me feel sad,
as if maybe she felt something more for me,
that i did not feel for her, and so i said, "sure,"
not knowing what else to say,
because it was midnight,
and the liquor was burning off
like stars inside my skull.

i watched her flipping pancakes
on the stove,
and she was barefoot,
wearing only an oversized shirt,
and i knew she should be making pancakes
for somebody else,
somebody who would want to read the paper
with her in the morning,

and make jokes with her about the president.
and i felt guilty for the pancakes,
and i didn't enjoy them,
even though they were soft,
and delicious,
and melted in my mouth.

I quit drinking
the very next day,
because I didn't ever want to feel
the sadness of pancakes
again.

poetry

    i was never good in English class, and hated poetry,
    the way it was taught like a foreign language,
    but when i first saw her walking down the halls,
    it lit a spark in me, made me feel things
    I could only describe in poetry,
    and so I wrote about her eyes
    "holding the light of Winter"
    or some such shit only a 16 year old can write.

My father once told me that he recited poetry
to my mother for three days before he won her heart,
but I didn't believe him. I didn't believe in the power of words,
until the day this girl finally let me kiss her,
just outside of the gym.
but instead of smiling,
she looked sad,
as if she were letting me down by giving in,
as if she held some secret tragedy
she didn't want to share,
as if she could already see the end in our beginning.

And so together we went through it all for just over a year,
the highs, the lows, the loss, and all the betrayals of youth,
making all the same mistakes as our parents
because it was the only playbook we had.

We fell apart word by word,
line by line,

until we were left as strangers again,
and if I had to sum us up in a poem for her,
I'd say,

We opened up a window
to let in the sunlight,
but just didn't count on the rain.

barrista

i met a girl at the coffee shop
and for three weeks we spoke about art,
and movies, and just how full of shit the world is,
and then we drank a couple beers at my place one night
and fucked on my green couch;
her body was pale and soft and graceful
in the red neon glow of hamburger light,
and for some reason in the middle of the pleasure
I felt a strange loss,
as if this was going to change things between us,
and break the mystery that kept us reading
by revealing too many clues.

afterward, i smoked a cigarette
and tried to smile.

I said I was sorry.

"for what?" she asked.

"i don't know," I said. "I felt like maybe I'd rushed you into this."

"you didn't rush me, Cash. if I didn't want to do this, I wouldn't have."

"yeah, i guess not," i said. "i don't know
what the fuck i am saying sometimes."

she laughed,
but then there was silence,
as the light outside switched from red to blue
but it was a beautiful blue,
as if we were underwater
and the sunlight
was trying to reach us,
but we were down too deep.

I lit another cigarette,
and laughed.

I didn't know
what else to do.

sellout

    We were at the party
    and i was trying to explain
    to my Mexican friend Javier
    that most Mexicans
    are more than just Indians
    but also Spanish in blood,
    but he didn't like that idea
    because he believed
    that Indians were pure
    and Europeans were evil
    and corrupt,
    and he brought up Columbus
    as an example,
    and I said,
    "but both of us have European is us too.
    I mean look at our skin,
    our jobs,
    our English.
    We are also part of the problem."

    "No," he said,
    "you are part of the problem."

    And I said,
    "I know I am, but so are you,"
    and then he said,

    "fuck you, you fucking sell out,"

and then he stormed out of the party
and into his new Volvo
which he had purchased
with funds from his job as a lawyer,
where he upholds the same laws
once used to kick Indians off their lands,
and I didn't know
whether to laugh or cry,
but I knew
when I got into my beat up Toyota,
I was still driving on the same highway
as him, paved by military experts
to make sure missiles could make it safely
across the country,
and that anybody in this country
who considered themselves pure,
and not a sell out,
better be living among the trees,
and the birds,
and hunting their own food
before they throw it
on the fire.

upgrades

It was hard enough
to make conversations
before these fancy phones arrived
with the tiny TV sets on them
where you can watch highlights
of the entire planet at all times.
And whereas before,
you could expect somebody
sitting across from you on the bus
to be just as bored as you,
staring out at the rain,
and wondering what it all means,
now you can bet they are
being entertained by something
far more interesting than the rain.

And now if you want to make the effort
to strike up a conversation
you risk pulling them away
from something far more interesting than you,
and your low bandwidth small talk,
and opinions on the weather.
furthermore,
instead of feeling good for
reaching across the void
of this long and lonely human existence
to try and make a connection,
you now feel like a pain in the ass.

Cash Carlos

So, if you want to talk to a stranger on the bus
or your sister or mother or kid,
it's better just to text them,
but just don't expect
a reply.

down

If you've ever been depressed,
you know what it's like
to feel as if nothing matters,
as if the world has gone from color
to black and white,
as the daily news stacks up
and there is no need to read it
because the rich are still rich,
and the poor are still poor,
and the horror is still horror.

So maybe you take a pill
to bring back the flowers
or you move to Mexico,
or you write poems to the wind,
but not even sadness can float on the sea forever,
and eventually sunlight falls
through the cracks of anything broken,
so you can't be sure of anything,
except life goes on.

And once you surrender to this,
you know better days are coming,
because all the horses in the race
are secretly yours.

coffee is cocaine light

i drank my coffee,
and felt the high that comes
with caffeine
and a new day,
and i believed I could solve
all the world's problems
if you gave me a pen
and a piece of paper,
but by noon,
the coffee was fading,
and I began to wonder
why anyone
in the world
would ever want
to talk to me or listen
to what I had to say
about anything
because i was a fraud,
and a nobody,
and that is when
I knew I needed
another cup
of coffee.

shallow

This one liked to do coke
and stay up all night painting,
big blotches of red and blue,
and after 3 days,
she'd fall asleep
exhausted with her own genius.

When we first met,
I liked her paintings
because I liked her,
and I imagined
these colorful explosions
is what my brain
would look like upon orgasm
with her,
but they turned out to be
more of the normal kind,
and meanwhile,
she lived on a trust fund,
and i had to keep working at the shoe store,
so i began to resent
coming home to her freedom of expression,
and prep school explanations
of a methodology that made no sense to me,
as she was, "trying to subvert the dominant paradigm
through feminist abstraction,"
and when finally she cheated
on me with another artist
who painted only female nudes,

and used her as his muse,
i told her that my turds
made more art than her,
and she laughed,
and said I would never understand,
because I was not a true artist,
and I said,
"I don't respect art
that anyone could do."
"How hard is it to
write about fucking?" she said.
"Hard," I said.
"You're just jealous," she said,
"because John Lucas has a bigger dick than you,"
and I said, "This has nothing to do with dicks.
this is about art that sucks dick,"
and lacking a better comeback than that,
I stormed out of the apartment,
and paced the neighborhood
for a good hour before returning
to find her gone. I packed my things,
and left her a note that said,
"I hope John Lucas visits you in rehab."
This was still the best I could do at the moment,
given that I was hurt and didn't know her
well enough to hurt her any deeper,
and I wanted to cry as I left,
to make it seem like we mattered,
but even that felt faked,
and lacking real art.

fuck it

Ever since I've gotten sober,
I've tried to live a better life,
be a better father, husband, and son,
but there comes a point when you realize
there's no end to improvement.

After you quit drinking,
they want you to pay the bills on time,
then organize your files,
and go to the gym. It is enough
to make a man want to drink.
So in order to stay sober
I read books by drunks and degenerates,
people who I can relate to.
people who remind me
it's okay to live life
without a million dollars
in the bank account.

It's okay to enjoy
a cup of coffee
in the park,
and watch the clouds pass.

It's okay to be sober,
and still live like a drunk.

pearl

I am getting my haircut
by a middle aged woman named Pearl,
and her voice is soothing me
like raspy notes played on an old record player,
as she tells me about her crazy parents
back in Arkansas, who told her not to move out here
where it always rains.

And I wonder how she can keep coming to work
now that her husband is gone,
and she's lost her kids to the drink.
How can she keep cutting hair for minimum wage,
with no other plans for the future
than to hit TJ's for wings after work.

I've still got my wife and kids,
and a job that doesn't suck my soul.
I quit drinking years ago,
but there are still days when I wonder
what the fuck I am doing,
and why in the fuck I keep going,
and it always comes back to the little things
like this,
listening to a strange woman
sing me the blues, as her gentle hand
strokes my forehead like an angel's wing,
bringing me back to earth.

detour

I didn't love her in the permanent kind of way.
And neither did she love me that way.
We knew we were pit stops,
and detours,
trails that sprawled off into the dark woods
that lead to some discovery.
We lived with each other,
ate together,
talked about music and movies.
and we fucked
to demolish the boredom and the routine,
to erase the work uniforms,
and slow all the ticking clocks in the world
demanding our time.

We were co-conspirators.
We were partners in crime.
We were temporary lovers,
waiting for the rain to stop,
and the blue sky to break.

When we finally said goodbye,
I wasn't even sad.

It was like saying thank you
to somebody
who helped you jump start your car
on the freeway.

Cash Carlos

We said goodbye,
knowing
there are still some good things in the world,
no one will ever know about
but us.

the beach

hot sand mixed with hope;
she's three tequilas into tomorrow
in a tight bathing suit,
as the big oily men
stream past her like balloons;
"She's mine," I think,
but she is not mine;
She is hers,
and I am pale
and skinny,
and not much of a fighter.

She says I make her laugh,
an adorable clown.

She asks if I want to put
some tanning cream on her back,
and I do.

I wink at the big oily men,
letting them know
this one is mine,
but she is not mine;
she belongs to the earth,
and the sky.

Cash Carlos

She belongs to Paris
and Rome,
and I am only a small town
without a name.
I am only a dreamer
on Holiday who
won a weekend cruise to Hawaii.
She is a waitress
I met on a Tuesday,
with nothing to lose.
We are six months of savings,
and a belief that sand and surf
will save us all.
I want to go back
to where it's cold.

I want to hide
behind the pie counter,
and drink myself to death.

she is an exotic bird
with feathers too bright to cage.
and she is a poet
who writes poems
with her body,
and reads Chaucer and Melville
on her cigarette break.

                                                continued

Dry Love

I have a degree in English,
and a job waiting tables
beside her,
so this is it for me.

She is going to college in the fall
and will not be mine for much longer,
so that night I make love to her like a fish
out of water,
and wait for the maid to knock
on the door
to tell us it's over.

the sunflower

The summer sun burned bright,
as the breeze blew through the windows,
and she lie naked on the bed,
reading a magazine,
and I wondered why there was famine,
death and war,
why kings never knew when to stop,
and armies fought
for gold they'd never see.

I kissed her
on the ass cheek,
gently stroked her breast,
and let history be.

time

we'd just fucked
in every position in the known universe,
from spider legs,
to a chili dog
and a side order of fries,
and I wanted to celebrate,
so i opened the window and sang
"We are the champions!" but the street
was quiet,
and there was only the sound
of a dog running out from behind a dumpster,
so i came back to bed,
where she was looking at her phone,
scrolling for memes and memories.
so i came to the typer to write this
and remember
all the glory
i felt this Friday night
in late June.
And in the silence
I could feel the the entire universe expanding
after cosmic orgasm,
also lonely,
and without much company.

after fucking

after fucking,
we'd discuss politics
and food,
but if she was still naked,
it didn't take long
for my mind
to begin wandering
back along
the contours
of her ass,
the bread of her breasts,
and soon
i was inside her again,
and fucking
the small talk away.

the glue that binds us

she's feeling sulky,
so she puts on the violin music
that fills the apartment with elegant melancholy,
and i know i will need at least three gin and tonics
just so i don't throw myself out the window.
And somewhere in the city
somebody is slitting their throat,
and somewhere a child is lost and crying,
and everything on the news is exploding,
and so i drink to anesthetize myself,
to the world with her in it;
i drink to find the oblivion inside me
that matches the oblivion on the walls,
the soulless art that soothes no one,
the pastel colors of hell she finds
in the latest catalogue;
she's bought a new dress,
and some jewelry.
she says we should go to Paris in June.
I turn on the television,
and pretend to pay attention to a cage fight on TV,
but i am dying inside,
so close, and so alone with death,
i can taste it.
"i'm sorry," i tell her, "we're done.
this can't go on."
she wants to know what and why.
"i can't explain it to you," i say,

"if i could, we wouldn't have this problem.
we wouldn't be listening
to violin music,
with our bones drenched in booze."

"who would we be then if
we were in love,"
she asks.

"i don't know," i say.
but we wouldn't be
us."

She turns off the TV
and goes to bed,
and the moon
follows her,
as if it has chosen
her side.

the green light

I remember when some of the girls
were attacking "The Great Gatsby" in class,
calling the main character a "creep,"
and the professor was trying to tell them
it was one of the greatest books of all time.
And though I had only read the SparkNotes,
I chimed in saying I thought the girls were right,
it was overrated
though I did like the idea of a man
trying to impress a woman
with his money and fancy clothes
because I myself had spent a large part of my paycheck
on a pair of Nike's that I thought
might catch the eye of a certain cheerleader in our class,
who was on the side of Gatsby,
and believed everything he did was romantic.
I shouldn't have been surprised
when my sneakers weren't enough to catch her attention,
and she went for a guy on the baseball team,
but unlike Gatsby, I didn't go on to then lie,
cheat and steal my way to a mansion and a pool.
I just accepted that some woman
aren't worth trying to impress,
and others will like you for who you are,
which may not be such a profound insight,
but I have been married now for many years,
and my wife has never complained
about us not living in a mansion,

Cash Carlos

and just like me,
she too believes Gatsby is overrated,
and his methods are absurd,
but the cheerleader in my class
went on to marry a man who is quite wealthy,
and last I heard she even lives by the ocean,
so maybe everyone gets what they're looking for in the end.

sleepwalkers

They never taught us in school
that the Nazi's did meth,
believed in dark magic,
and made lampshades
from the skin of children;

They showed us the crisp uniforms,
pep rallies, and confetti. and maybe
one or two shots of skeletons
in the dirt. before they put us to sleep
with numbers and statistics
that sounded like math class.

They should have kept the horror
in the story,
and reminded us how some monsters
can't be killed
because their ideas
still walk the earth like ghosts,
waiting to rise again.

I would have gotten an A in history.

I would have stayed wide awake.

Cash Carlos
a poem for my daughter

After one day sober, everything hurts,
but even when life seems so fucked
there's nothing you can do but get up,
shove in some eggs,
and drink coffee like a drunk,
as you do your best to fake a smile.

There will still be moments when the clouds break
and you'll see some kid playing in the park,
reminding you there are many worlds
inside this one,
secret places where music and laughter live
in perpetual revolution of a heart,
and with time and tears,
you can live to feel young again.
and the past will no longer matter.

It will be like a memory of one day when it hurt,
and the next day it didn't.

Just be patient, drink coffee,
and wait for it.

adjunct professor

Today in poetry class,
we talked about the difference between art
and business and why sometimes superficial shit
sells like a hotcakes
while quality remains on a shelf collecting dust;
Then, somebody quoted Miles Davis as saying,
"Man, it takes a long time to sound
like yourself," and I thought, "fuck, isn't that the truth,
especially when it's so easy to copy the sound
of another."

Then, a woman with a tattoo of a mermaid
between her breasts told us
about how her husband committed suicide last year,
and how she didn't want his death to sound cliche,
and I thought of the death of my father,
and said, "Death has its own timeline, I think,
and it makes its own rules, so it doesn't matter
how you write about it, as long as you do."

And it was right about this time an alarm went off,
and a loudspeaker told us that somebody
had reported an emergency in the building
and I said, "Ten years ago,
I would have made jokes and kept reading poems,
but now,
with so many lunatics shooting up
schools, we should get the fuck out."

Cash Carlos

And so we went outside,
and it was raining,
and nobody saw flames or heard the sound of bullets,
and it all all smelled of a false alarm,
so we started joking around,
and one student had a skateboard,
so I tried to do an ollie but failed,
but they were delighted I,
the old instructor, had tried,
and more delighted when i cracked a joke
saying, "Tomorrow the newspaper
will show a picture of me on a skateboard,
headlined, "Instructor Skateboards,
While Students Burn In Flames,"
and everyone laughs,
and their eyes look brighter,
washed of the classroom grey,
and I felt like we were all young again,
thankful just to be alive,
and that any moment now,
there would be a voice coming over the loudspeaker,
telling us it was safe to go back inside.

dear cash, we're sorry

I send in poems for publication,
and they tell me my writing is too simple,
and too much about fucking,
but i like fucking poems,
and use simple words by choice,
but they want Spanish revolutions and roses,
fields of flowers bedded to an azure sky;
they want Chopin and Keats,
and obscure references in Latin and Greek.

I know what they want,
but I can't give it to them
because it's not my style,
so I keep feeding myself these poems
full of dusty boots,
and the thin boned women of my youth.
these temporary tattoos who left by morning,
without kisses, flowers, or poetry,
and even if they never came back,
i never forgot them.

i kept part of them in my heart,
and in my poems,
even if all I get back
are rejection slips
in return.

ice age

From the age of 16 to 26,
I used to grab a drink or a smoke
anytime I felt an emotion,
but after a while I became frozen
and couldn't feel a thing.

So I quit it all,
just to make sure I was real,
and slowly began to defrost
like an ancient wooly mammoth,
encased in a block of ice.

I started to feel and re-feel
one emotion at a time,
sometimes laughing,
sometimes sobbing,
sometimes staring at the wall,
as I lumbered on two weary legs
all the way into present day,
with a raw
and endangered heart.

you know nothing of paris

"You know nothing of Paris, son,"
my father said, taking a drink of scotch,
and adjusting his tie,
"until you've made love to a Parisian girl
along the banks of the Seine after so much wine,
cheese, and French poetry
that you forget the world of color,
and everything, including the rain,
turns the black and white
of an old postcard…"

"Wow," i said. "Not bad."

"i am not finished," he said,
"you enter a sad cafe
together, holding hands,
looking lost and soaked
as she reaches over to touch your cheek,
kisses you, and gently,
pulls out your heart
and presses it between the pages
of the last book of poetry
you'll ever read."

My father lifts his scotch to me, winks,
and says, "you can quote me on that."

milk for breakfast

It's late Saturday night
and I'm getting milk for tomorrow's breakfast
at the 7-Eleven
and in walks this blonde girl, slightly tossed,
asking for Marlboro lights.
and her hair is like spun gold,
and her clothes are impeccable
and I can tell just by the way she walks
she lives in a different world to me,
and I can see her boyfriend
waiting for her impatiently in a black BMW
worth more than all the cars
I've ever owned put together,
and he looks barely 21,
while I'm already
middle-aged and married,
and perfectly content with my milk
and my piece of shit Toyota
that's invisible to them,
but I can tell the boyfriend
is getting impatient on his phone
and by the time she gets into the car,
she wants to know who called.
and why he won't show her the number
as the night grows long,
for even the beautiful, the privileged,
and the rich.

the happiest place on earth

i went to disneyland once as a kid,
and i can remember the magic,
how each submarine and car
was kid-sized and waiting just for me,
but the next time I went I was 23,
and still drinking heavy like my father;
i had just dropped out of college,
and as I stood in line,
waiting an hour for a two minute ride,
I couldn't help but marvel at all the lonely people,
with skinned knees and cameras,
mouse-cars, fat bellies, and blank looks on their faces,
and I thought this is capitalism in a nutshell;
working and waiting joylessly
for a few seconds of fun,
and then it's over, they kick you out,
and tell you to come back when you have more money.
i remember how hard it was for me to smile
even when the roller coaster whipped me around
in the dark,
and I wondered, very seriously, what was wrong with me,
and why i went to college at all,
when all it taught me was to see through the lens
of class struggle, and opression.

i went back to Disneyland the last time at 35,
married with kids,
stone cold sober and humbled by life's unrelenting tide;
(my father already dead from the drinking disease).

and this time I can see the world
through the eyes of my seven year old son.
i see the wonder, the mystery,
the beauty, and the promise,
but even with all the rides,
and attractions,
my favorite part of the day
was walking through the parking lot at dusk,
sober with my son on my back,
feeling his small hands in mine,
and knowing this means more.

the wine of youth

My wife and I get invited to a pool party
by a young woman from my work,
and jesus she's a looker;
a buxom blonde,
twenty years younger than my wife,
she answers the door in a skimpy yellow bikini;
her curves remind me of the Swiss Alps,
and yodeling, and I don't want my wife
to think I am ogling her,
so I keep my eyes up high,
and smile as we're lead out to the pool.

This is when my wife whispers,
 "Jesus, did you see her tits? I couldn't help
ogling them."
I laugh, and we sit down at a table
with some chips and tepid salsa,
and look around for somebody
to talk to aside from ourselves.
Most of the guests are younger,
in their late twenties or early thirties,
and this is when I remember why
we never come to things like this.
Even though I get a kick out of young people,
they live in a different world,
a shark tank of competition
and cunning,
where every move is calculated
toward rising another notch on the ladder of success.

Cash Carlos

My wife was 29 when we first met,
and I still don't miss
the ways when she would get
ogled by every horny dick on the highway.

There is something relaxing about
marriage and middle age,
and being content with where you are.
You have no more need
for posturing or preening,
dick swinging or tit flaunting.

And so we make polite small talk,
and a few jokes about the weather
before walking out the door.
and maybe it was all the perfume
and pheromones that rouses us,
reminds of when we were younger,
and still fucked for sport,
but my wife's grabbing at my crotch,
and the music on the stereo is playing something
that hauls us back in time.

We end up pulling off by the side of the road
for a quickie in a church parking lot,
so all in all it ends up being
a very good day.

i still get high

I still get high on magazines and coffee,
laundry piles and instant messages
from the grave.
I still get high on traffic jams,
and burrito stands,
college girls walking like angels
into the wind.

I still get high on her body,
and the way it never stops
calling my name.

I still get high on sobriety
and anxiety, failure,
and vitamins
with purported hidden powers.

I still get high on bad news,
rabbit holes,
and conspiracies
that are declassified too late.

I still inhale the day
like a Colombian fatty
and let the fire
burn me like an ant
beneath a magnifying glass,

Cash Carlos

as my hollow shell
coils into colors
too intricate to name,
and when
the end comes
I will disappear
inside them,
wanting more.

likes and follows

There was a girl I knew in school named Rita
who was always ahead of her time.
she had tattoos of flames on her back
and wore faded jeans torn at the knees.
She could talk about revolution,
Leonard Cohen and Kurt Cobain.
To me she was like a mystery
rolled into a joint and smoked by Jesus
to make the rain clouds,
until last week,
when,
after 15 years of wondering
what happened to her,
she friended me on Facebook,
then posted a picture of a meatloaf
that looked just like everybody else's.

sunday

We make good love,
and I feel like we've conquered the world,
and there's nothing left to do or accomplish,
prove,
or earn;
presidents and legacies die
in lonely castles of gold,
as soldiers write love letters stained in blood.
I listen to her breathing,
feel her body with the tips of my fingers,
and let my eyes imagine things in the ceiling,
bullfighters,
tsunamis,
telephone lines riddled with birds.
I can hear the sound of a million lonely lies
all dying
in the darkness. The phone rings,
and I don't answer.

Everything that matters
is already here.

superman

Cleaning out my desk at work today
I found a picture of a superhero
my son drew for me when he was five
and needed to come to work with me
for reasons I can't remember.

And I felt a longing in my gut,
and wished he was with me now,
because of how quickly time passes
from innocence to experience,
and sometimes I don't know
if my sadness is for missing time with him
or me wishing I'd had more time
with my own father before he died
or if it even matters.

I'm proud of the young man
my son has become and the father
I've been to him, but it still hurts
to love somebody so much,
knowing one day
you'll have to let them go,
but that's just life,
and nobody escapes it.

I will never stop caring for my son
as he grows into a man,
but it's never the same

as when they were young
and you could hold them in your arms,
and it was so easy to know
what love looks like.

About Cash Carlos

Cash Carlos is an unpublished poet from the Pacific Northwest who writes sober about being drunk, and writes about one night stands while being wed to one woman. He writes to entertain and educate his own soul. Part Irish, part Colombian, all American, he also enjoys skateboarding, cage fights, cooking, travel, donuts, yerba mate, typewriters, basset hounds, bicycles, Frida Kahlo, Basquiat, Raymond Carver, James Baldwin, Gabriel Garcia Marquez, hippos, The Office, Breaking Bad, Game of Thrones, Ludwig Wittgenstein, Albert Camus, bukowski, Russell Edson, Amy Winehouse, Gloria Anzaldua, Noam Chomsky, Pamela Anderson, Bruce Lee, Salvador Dali, Paulo Freire, Carl Jung, The Dead Kennedys, Jodorowsky, Prince, Kanye, Mark Gonzales, Dave Chappelle, Alfonsina Storni, Bill Hicks, Kurt Cobain, and tacos.

Made in the USA
Monee, IL
30 August 2021